"ROYALTY"

IMPACT!
Publishing Co.

KTP-Impact Publishing

PO Box 691533 Charlotte NC 28227

For more Information visit
www.DevelopingQueens.Com

DevelopingQueens@gmail.com

"ROYALTY"

ROYALTY
"In Pursuit Of
THE CROWN"

Dr. DeNae LeMay

CONTENTS

DEDICATION

To my Eternal Lord, Savior and lover of my soul, Jesus The Christ: I thank you for entrusting me with the responsibility of sharing your relational truth with the world.

To my amazing husband of 28 years Dr. Stacy LeMay, whose steadfast love, commitment, passion and resiliency in the Kingdom of God continues to be the well by which I drink from. Thank you for demonstrating what a KINGDOM MAN truly looks like.

To my four gifts, my offspring, the fruit of my womb, my loving children; Christian, Uriah, Jasmine and Benny: Through the many years your childlike faith and trust in me, placed a demand on my life which has caused me to soar higher, press harder, and to believe greater. Always know that being your mother will always be my greatest joy in this life! I love you all more than words can express.

To my precious mother, the late Ira Jean James: my very first teacher and the most virtuous role model I have ever known. Though our time together was brief, I am Eternally grateful for the life you modeled before me. To my one and only sister Jeanease, always know that I love you dearly.

To Dr. Gloria Williams, thank you for always sharing your wisdom and for being a solid pillar of consistent Faith and enduring Strength.

To the late Dr Myles and Pastor Ruth Munroe: Thank you for your endless hours of mentoring and for helping me understand that teaching the Kingdom does not come without a weight of responsibility. I cherish the many lessons you taught and demonstrated before me. Thank you for revealing to me and the world how true Royalty Carries the Crown.
TO THE KING!

To all the women whom have come to realize that their purpose has significance, I sound the alarm and cry aloud to you…
it's time to ARISE, EMERGE and PURSUE YOUR DESTINY! Your worth is greater than you could have ever imagined.

May you always remember that you are ROYALTY!
Go Now! and pursue your crown!

Dr. DeNae LeMay

FOREWORD

Dr. DeNae LeMay has written a very inciteful book that portrays the making and understanding of what it means to be a family member of The Royal Class. As we take the journey through the pages of this book we see the results of total commitment and dedication, to following God's pattern of the royal family life. Dr. DeNae shares many of her own personal life experiences that added to her inevitable decision to pursue her Royal Purpose.

She reveals and expresses how important it is to have the knowledge of who God says we are, no matter what anyone else has to say.

Image-building is clearly a branding of

Dr. DeNae's book,

"Royalty In Pursuit of The Crown".

I highly endorse and recommend this material as a very good read for study groups.

Dr. Gloria Williams

Jesus People Ministries Miami, Fl

<u>ENDORSEMENTS</u>

A TRUE WOMAN OF ROYALTY

There was a time when women were taught, trained, and groomed to be and act like a lady. There was an expectation of modesty and self-respect demonstrated by the way a young lady dressed, and the way she represented herself through careful speech. Our culture today is the very opposite, stained with women who exhibit wild behavior, vulgar speech, lude and provocative dress. What was once looked as detestable now fills the racks of almost every trendy women's clothing store.

With the popularity of YouTube videos that place emphasis on the importance of contouring your make-up, the new eye lash extensions, hair weave tutorials, and eyebrow arching, the importance of character building has been significantly pushed down the list.

This stark reality leaves the state of our young and elder women in a desperate need of a mothering voice. A voice that is not afraid, a voice that is bold, a voice that not only represents in word only, but in action. Today's women need a Royal model, which leads me to believe that we are in desperate need of a model Dr. DeNae LeMay. A woman with such a powerful voice that is graced with knowledge and wisdom. Dr. DeNae is clearly a modern-day Proverbs 31 woman. One that is classy yet powerful, bold yet gentle, a mentor, a powerful speaker, a loving mother, a supportive wife, a First Lady, and moreover, a confident, Kingdom Woman of God.

With her multiple complex roles, she somehow manages to exude ROYALTY every time she steps into a room. Her Royal roots run deep in her veins, poised with integrity, graced with strong character, and her captivating presence helps you to realize, you have just been in company with a Queen.

I believe that Dr. DeNae LeMay was birthed into this generation for the specific purpose of developing Queens for the Kingdom of God. I am confident that this book is sure to unveil secrets and will reveal to women of all ages their identity in Christ, and as Royal Women of God. This book is certain to Equip the reader with the tools needed to properly pursue the very nature, character, and integrity of a Woman of Royalty. Get ready to be filled with truth. I promise you, Your life will never be the same again after reading this book.

Toy Banks

Author/Public speaker

Better Wife Better Life

Dr. DeNae LeMay is a Kingdom focused woman of God who has inspired many through exemplary leadership, spiritual insight and motivation. Her insights on Royalty as it relates to the women in the Kingdom are powerful and illuminating. With a focus on developing women who pursue value over vanity and character over charisma, Dr. DeNae redirects women to pursue what is truly valuable and lasting, a relationship with the King which in turn guarantees all the desires of the heart righteously.

Dr. Dave Burrows

Author/ Sr. Pastor Bahamas Faith Ministries International

After nearly 30 years of marriage to this amazing woman of virtue, I can confidently confirm that there is no one more qualified to write a book on such a topic than Dr. DeNae LeMay. Her consistent demonstration of Confidence, Courage and Royal Class behavior is a model for all to see and must be reproduced for many generations to come. Not only is she an elegant, kind and caring model of motherhood, but her relentless example as a supportive wife and loyal friend could be used as a prototype not only to shape families, but to shape nations. It is my great honor to endorse this riveting book filled with such anointed and Royal wisdom. However, the greatest gift I treasure, is the privilege I have to spend the rest of my days in the same company of a Queen.

To My Lovely,
Dr. Stacy A LeMay

<u>INTRODUCTION</u>

Every woman likes **ROYALTY** but only a few know how to Reign! Royalty is the part in which most women will embrace in the pursuit because it is the most attractive and can be visibly seen. After all, who would refuse a life filled with grandeur, wealth, honor and fairytale endings? With the most recent Royal wedding of America's princess Meghan Markel to Prince Harry, Duke of Sussex, there was much chatter, conversation and excitement about their enchanting wedding. The dress, her hairstyle, the venue, the type of flowers, the celebrity guest list and reception festivities. These are all things that would make us beam with excitement and leap with joy. Yet how many women truly understand the cost that is required in such a Royal pursuit? Not just in financial expense but the costly sacrifice Meghan had to consider in every area of her life. Oh yes, she married the man of her dreams, Her knight in shining armor.

However, she did so with the full understanding of Great **PRIVILEGE** and Great **RESPONSIBILITY.** I like to think of it this way…..

Princess Meghan *"had to exchange what she had become in order to become who she was destined to be."*
Dr. DeNae LeMay

I believe this is the realization that each of us must come to. Understanding that there is a *Process* and **Responsibility** attached to the *Privilege* of wearing *THE CROWN*. Every woman pursuing ROYALTY must always Remember this,

"All those who desire to wear the crown should also become comfortable with living an uncommon life."
Dr. DeNae LeMay

Your choices will be uncommon.
Your relationships will be uncommon.
Your disciplines will be uncommon.

Your walk with God will definitely be uncommon.

Having said this, I send a clarion call to all women, regardless of your background, education, economic standing, age or color *You are called to live a life of Royalty.*

This call goes out to every woman, However, please allow me to ask you a question in conjunction with the call. The Question is simply this....are you **prepared** to answer the call of ROYALTY?

Before you answer my question, please allow me to say that not answering the call would be the equivalent of being selected for a starring role in a major Broadway production, yet because of the **responsibility** associated with the role, you would rather choose to be the understudy!

Let me Inform you that

"Life doesn't give you what you want, Life gives you what you fight for!"
Dr. DeNae LeMay

If you don't **contend** for the crown you will settle for looking at it instead of obtaining the crown! I would like to share a statement my husband, Dr. Stacy LeMay shared with me. This statement was my motivation for writing this book.

He said

"DeNae, always remember that no matter who, nor how many people choose to discontinue, there will always remain a REMNANT!"

This statement is so simple yet so profound and accurate. No matter how many walk away from the pursuit there will always remain those who will count the cost, contend and remain in it to win it! I believe that there will always be a **Royal Remnant** who will keep their eyes on the crown and have already counted the cost. I believe there will always be those who are willing to pay the price, in order to accomplish the assignment they were given birth to fulfill in the earth. These are women who are determined to make a significant world-Impacting deposit within their lifetime. These women are aware that if they are to make a lasting impact in this life, they must not cast off what has been entrusted to them like a worn-out pair of shoes. Instead they must stay focused, be determined and remain in **diligent pursuit of the crown.** This Royal Remnant of women understand that obtaining their prize will require diligent *pursuit, process* and *responsibility.*

The Royal Remnant recognize that they are not only responsible for themselves, but for the whole area of leadership in which they have been assigned to Reign. As we move into the upcoming chapters and draw closer to the secrets to obtaining the crown, there is something I need you to understand.

"Royalty will require of you, responsibilities are expected of you, and diligent pursuit is necessary to Rule and Reign!"
Dr. DeNae LeMay

My hope in writing this book is that it will ignite an infectious flame within a remnant of women that will give birth to life impacting vision, burn with passionate desire to see beyond their current situation and stir up boldness to RISE WITH STRENGTH to pursue the crown.

Ladies! Our world needs you,
our communities need you, our families need you and most importantly, The King needs you!
Say yes to the call, commit to the pursuit of royalty and prepare to WEAR YOUR CROWN!
Shall we begin?

CHAPTER 1

ROYALTY

Always hold yourself to a higher standard than anyone else expects of you.
~ Dr. DeNae LeMay

You are a chosen people, a royal priesthood, a holy nation, God's special possession that you may declare the praises of him who called you out of darkness into his wonderful light.

1Peter 2:9 MSG

I have an announcement for you! One that you may have never considered before. This announcement, whether you know it, agree with it, or even believe it, this announcement is true and it's about you! It's an announcement that I can't wait to share with you. It's only three words but three very powerful words. These words carry much weight and great authority. When you hear these words, they will cause you to rethink who you really are. For when you understand the magnitude of these words nothing will be able to stop you! Can you imagine what these three words are? Are you ready to hear them? The three words I've been excited to share with you are these...

YOU ARE ROYALTY"!

Yes, I said it and I'll say it again, "YOU ARE ROYALTY"! These are three simple words yet when spoken and believed, they release tremendous Kingdom authority, power and dominion for the woman that is truly hearing them.

When you hear the word royalty most people think of Buckingham palace, Prince William, Prince Harry and their wives, horse drawn carriages with tradition and protocol. Yes, it's true that all these things represent the lifestyle of royalty, but what truly is Royalty? There are many definitions for the word Royalty, but the Cambridge dictionary has the most Kingdom-focused definition. The Cambridge dictionary defines Royalty as *"the people who belong to the family of a king or queen"*. Simplistic, yet I love this definition best because it exemplifies the heart of The King toward His daughters. We are His daughters; the apple of His eye and we belong to Him. We are a part of His family and He cares so much for us that He has called us sons and daughters and heirs to the promise. We are a part of the royal family which makes us royalty! We are joint-heirs with Jesus and are accepted in the beloved. Our Father is The King! Creator of Heaven and Earth and we are His Royal seed. You must believe that this is who you truly are! This is your inheritance! This is what He's called and created you to be! Isn't that great news? So many women today struggle with believing this, because religion has done a great job of training us to think of ourselves as slaves of God instead of sons and daughters of God. Romans 8:15-17 tells us exactly who we are.

Romans 8:15-17 NIV

[15] The Spirit you received does not make you slaves, so that you live in fear again; rather, the Spirit you received brought about your adoption to sonship. And by him we cry,

"Abba, Father." [16] The Spirit himself testifies with our spirit that we are God's children. [17] Now if we are children, then we are heirs---heirs of God and co-heirs with Christ, if indeed we share in his sufferings in order that we may also share in his glory.

How do you see yourself?

Self-image is something most women, young and old come to deal with at some point in their lives. Ranging from CEO's to housewives across all lines of economics, education, color and faith beliefs, women are searching to understand and know their significance and purpose on the earth. We all simply want to know, "Who am I and what am I assigned to do?" Validation, confirmation and understanding of who you are in Christ is essential to becoming a woman of Royalty.

Growing up, I never considered myself as royalty and I certainly never thought of myself as being from a royal family. I personally grew up in a small country town where everyone cared for everyone like family. The living was easy, and life was so much simpler back then. I lived in a town where you could smell the aroma of fresh baked rolls or fried chicken blowing in the breeze from the neighbor's house. My high school graduating class, according to today's standard, was considered a very small class. We graduated under 75 students and although college was talked about, not many in my class were able to make that dream a reality. Growing up in a single-wide mobile home and having to drive 35 minutes or more to the nearest grocery store, a girl can become accustomed to her environment and think only to the level of what she has been exposed to. However, *my mother*, who was an elementary school teacher, would not allow me to become so complacent. Instead she constantly pushed and involved me in as many activities as she could afford. My mother sacrificed tremendously in order to provide me with opportunities that would help to expand my mind and exposure. What she was doing was planting seeds for ideas and dreams to grow inside of me. I thank God tremendously for my mother. Although I did not have her on earth with me as long as I would have desired, she taught me many lessons and left memories that will remain with me for my entire life. My Mother transitioned when I was only 21 years old. I think of her often, wishing she were here. She was such an amazing woman! It's powerful to look back and see the impact of every seed she deposited into my life! She was, without a doubt, my catalyst. She was the spark that started my pursuit for purpose in life and she fed my hunger to know who I am as a daughter of God and a woman of Royalty.

Though the years following her transition were extremely difficult, the hardest challenge was not only in her physical absence but the sudden decrease of volume in hearing her words. During my childhood she was the only one who spoke to my identity, worth and value. Now that she is no longer here, it didn't take long for me to realize that

"I had to pursue the one she taught about in order to become the one she talked about."

I knew what she said about me, but it was time for me to learn what God said about me. I knew there was more to learn about my identity. I also knew that in order to live a Kingdom life I must believe, by faith, what God Himself has spoken through His word in order to become Royalty.

I believe that I need to pause here for a moment and say to you… your Heavenly Father does not want you to question if you are Royalty, He wants you to KNOW that you are Royalty! He has a wonderful inheritance for you and He's waiting for you to accept your position as a royal priesthood in His Kingdom. Let me ask you a question… "Are you living a life of Royalty?" If not, what's holding you back?

Could it possibly be the way that you're thinking? Could it possibly be what your believing in your heart and mind? Could it possibly be the people in your life that want you to think otherwise? If so, this next section is just for you. Let us continue.

THINK LIKE ROYALTY

Have you ever been invited to attend an event where perhaps you felt like saying,

"How in the world did I get here? "

You know, an event that made you feel awkward or uncomfortable? Sounds like something we all have been a part of, right? Well, I know I sure have. The first thing I do when I'm in those positions is to pull my thoughts together and remind myself of WHO I AM and WHOSE I AM. I must think like Royalty, speak like Royalty and carry myself with Royalty. Then I remind myself that I AM ROYALTY and as a ROYAL, I am here to represent, first and foremost, my Heavenly Father, and I am to fulfill His will and assignment in the earth. When we remind ourselves that we are royalty, then we will behave like royalty no matter where He sends us. Could you imagine princess Meghan, Duchess of Sussex, at an event around non-royals sitting in a corner somewhere, or worse, walking around with her head down between her legs, exemplifying such embarrassing and non-royal behavior? Certainly not!

Now granted, she has only been in the royal family for a short period of time but from the onset of the announcement of her engagement she has been expected to behave as if she has grown up in the palace. Well, I believe our Heavenly Father expects the same of us. In His word he calls us heirs and joint-heirs with Jesus

Christ. He has made available to us, every resource that we may need in order to live life to the full in overflow and abundance.

He knows, like princess Meghan, we didn't grow up in the palace but were adopted into this privilege. He knows that everything we do and say may be scrutinized and judged harshly by accusers. That's why He's given us the Holy Spirit to help us, to teach us and guide us through every situation we may encounter. One thing I have learned from these experiences is that when you take on the mindset of royalty, others seem to know it too. Even if they are unable to correctly articulate it, they simply know there is something unique and special about you. When you start believing in the royalty you possess, others will seek you out for your words of encouragement, input and wisdom.

I am always amazed by the King's divine appointments, as I like to call them. God has many of them set up for us daily.

It's amazing how a simple trip to Walmart or the grocery store or even to the doctor's office can turn into an opportunity to demonstrate royalty in action. Whenever He gives you an opportunity to demonstrate His principles of love, grace and character to individuals that He sends your way, be sure that you do it!

Royalty thinks consistently of how they can best represent and expand the interest of their country. Have you ever shared the goodness of God with someone and noticed how they press in for more as you intrigue them with wisdom from above?

That's because you're displaying the power of The Kingdom. The Kingdom of God is God's way of doing things in the earth and His desire is for everyone to hear about it. The Kingdom brings power over circumstances and enables everyone the opportunity to embrace solutions to the many problems which are prevalent in the world. The Kingdom provides answers to questions and encouragement to despair. There's no greater joy than seeing a darkened heart receive light as it becomes radically changed for the work of God. Wouldn't you agree? I Believe that when we start doing Matthew 6:33, *seek first the Kingdom of God and His righteousness and all these things will be added to you*, we will be less consumed by what's happening to us, because we are focusing on what He's doing in and through us.

Royalty thinks differently.

Where others see problems, royalty sees solutions. Where others feel fear, royalty walks in faith.

Royalty learns from wisdom not from experience only. Royalty always thinks in a way that is higher than the standard.

Have you ever heard the saying, "experience is the best teacher"? Well, let me be the first to inform you that experience is not always the best teacher. Ask someone who has been through a bankruptcy. Do you believe that bankruptcy is the best teacher for a person to learn about money management? I can hear some of you say, "Dr. Denae, I've been through a bankruptcy and I learned so much. I grew up, I became better with money." I would say yes, I believe you did. I believe you may have learned the lesson but was that the "BEST" teacher for that lesson? Certain lessons force us to do what we would not do. I know there are exceptions and I can hear those exceptions talking back to me, but it usually comes down to this. If we would sit at the feet of Wisdom, we will learn the lessons she is desiring to teach us.

Let me share a story with you. When queen Victoria was a child, she didn't know she was in line for the throne of England. Her instructors, trying to prepare her for the future, were frustrated because they couldn't motivate her. She just didn't take her studies seriously. Finally, her teachers decided to tell her that one day she was to become queen of England. Upon hearing this, Victoria quietly said, "then I will be good." The realization that she would inherit this high calling gave her a sense of responsibility that profoundly affected her conduct from that point on. Just like Queen Victoria, many of us are in line for greatness. We are women of royalty, with a great inheritance, yet far too many squander their inheritance, which costs them so much lost time, purpose and destiny. Like Queen Esther, you are not being sent to the palace for your own benefit but for a greater purpose. We have not been placed in this position, this city, this assignment, this church, this family only for our personal dreams and desires to be fulfilled, but for God's will to be done on earth as it is in heaven.

Royalty gives intentional thought to the resources it has been entrusted with. Royalty likes to think more in line with use and not waste. Even Jesus after he fed the 5000 not including women and children, said "gather up the fragments that remain." (John 6:12)

It may have looked like waste but to Jesus it was necessary to gather it up. Let me encourage you to remember this wisdom, **"Never overlook what is left".**

There's something powerful and valuable in that which **REMAINS.** Set this into your subconscious mind and recall it daily. That will help kickstart your tomorrow with great success. Even if it's difficult to discern, ask God to reveal the resources that remain and show you how to use those resources for His glory. The most valuable resources, such as time, treasure and talent, are always looking to fulfill their responsibility and assignment.

The media was so intrigued with Meghan Markel, Duchess of Sussex, and all the decisions she would have to make regarding her current lifestyle. There was much conversation swirling through the media as they questioned if she would say goodbye to all she had known and loved in order to marry the man of her dreams. Her decision may have been difficult, but she was ready to embrace the greater good that was ahead of her. I believe she gave great thought to her decision in marrying Prince Harry. The thought of giving up her career, comforts, family and all she has known in order to follow her heart came with careful and great consideration. I believe she understood this one simple fact, that

"sometimes you must give up who you are in order to become who you were truly destined to be"!

Her story, as remarkable as it is, cannot begin to measure up to the amazing life God has prepared for you! You are a part of the royal family with full support of the Kingdom at your request. The King will make sure your destiny (which was *"prepared before the foundations of the world"* Eph 1:4) is fulfilled! His promise is that all your needs have been supplied by His riches in glory by Christ Jesus. Allow me to remind you that you're the apple of His eye, His joy and His delight. If you have yet to do so at this time, I invite you to take the next step in this royal process and pursue your amazing destiny by first Pursuing the King.

CHAPTER 2

What's your pursuit?

Pursuits are good when they take you in the right direction.
~ Dr. DeNae LeMay

In life, there are many pursuits that we will embark upon. Things that we passionately go after. Things that we see as valuable for our lives such as education, relationships, careers, finances and goals. We believe that these things are necessary and many of them are, yet we should make sure that we prioritize our pursuits according to their highest value.

Believe it or not, pursuit is something we all have in common. **Although we may not be in pursuit of the same things, we**

are all in pursuit of something. According to Webster's dictionary,

Pursuit is defined as the act of following something, either to catch it or to engage it.
Pursuit is also defined as an interest to which a person devotes their time and energy.

If you turn on the television or watch any form of social media today, it doesn't take a seasoned Prophet to discern what women are pursuing these days. The spectrum is as numerous as there are days in the year. Everything from money, wealth-building, developing fame, parenting, status, branding, relationships, marriage, education, career, leisure, emotional fulfillment, just to name a few. I could continue but I believe you get the point here which is this, **"everyone is in pursuit of something"**.
Now I can hear some of you ask, "Dr. Denae, what's wrong with pursuing these things?" Is it wrong to go after your

dreams or your goals?" My response is "certainly not", as long as what you are pursuing keeps the heart, will and desire of God first. So often we forget that as citizens of the Kingdom of God, we have chosen by an act of our will, to accept and allow **the Lord- which means owner** -to lead and instruct our lives. Did you know that when you made the decision from living life "without Him" to living life "for Him", you agreed to give the Lord access and authority in the decision -making process of your life? That's why as Royalty, our first pursuit should be for our King. When we press in to maintain a consistent pursuit of His presence, it will enable us to know His heart and mind concerning every area of our lives.

When we pursue His thoughts, we learn His will and ultimately fulfill the destiny He has prepared for us from the foundations of the world.

Psalms 119:10 (message translation) says; I'm single-minded in pursuit of You. Don't let me miss the road signs You've posted.

I love this translation because it speaks not only to the pursuit but to making sure that we are aware and in right alignment with the pursuit we are after. Often, we pursue things/goals that we were never designed to pursue. Which is a mere waste of time, effort and resources. How many times have we stopped, looked around and seen that we were on life's highway, going north when we should have been going South. Yet, because we've spent so much time, energy and effort in "this" direction we find it more comfortable to remain on that course then to stop, turn around and go in the direction that we should be heading. I'd like to say it this way;

"Pursuits are good when they take you in the right direction."

Let me ask you a question, have you ever been on your way to a destination only to find out that you were going in the wrong direction? Well, if it hasn't happened to you it surely has happened to me and I'd like to share one of those moments with you.

One of my greatest joys in life is being a mother. I love it! I have been blessed with four beautiful children. I have three gifted sons (Christian, Uriah and Benjamin) and one amazing daughter named Jasmine. I have truly enjoyed the seasons of motherhood from those "trying two's" to those "Momma gonna knock you out" teen years! Lol. The carpool rides, homeschooling days (yes, I said homeschool!) extracurricular activities and serving in our local church, has always kept us quite busy. Now, I don't want you to think that because I said I enjoyed these years that everything was peaches and cream or that I lived a "Beaver Cleaver" life. No, not by a long shot. However, what I want to share is that I have enjoyed raising, developing, nurturing, guiding and most importantly, loving these four gifts given by God to my husband and me. All my children have played sports. My three sons have all enjoyed one sport more than any other and that's football. In fact, all three of them have attained All-American status while playing football. During their high school years, the summer and fall months were always very busy for us. Between taking them to and from practices, workouts, meetings, team meals, volunteering for concession stands not to mention school, work and ministry. In the midst of juggling all these activities, things could get a little hectic. One thing that helped ease the load was our excitement for "Friday night lights".

WE ABSOLUTELY LOVED IT! We loved the smell of fresh cut grass on a crisp Friday fall evening. There's nothing like the sound of the band warming up and the blare of the referee's whistle. Seeing the faces of cheering fans and the smell of stadium treats from the concession stand, it made us feel like we're at our second home. Now, I'm not one of those yelling / screaming football moms but I do get a little excited from time to time. Well... most of the time, well... actually every game, Lol. My husband, my daughter and I generally traveled to the games together. However, on this occasion, I had a meeting to attend and had to travel alone. Because I had been to this stadium before, I didn't feel the need to ask for directions. I even remember saying to my husband, "I know how to get there. I'll be good". Well, after my meeting I began to travel in the direction of my "pursuit" and as I was traveling, I realized that nothing looked familiar. I told myself "Just keep going. You're not close enough that's why you don't recognize anything. When You get closer, you'll recognize some of the signs." Well, guess what happened? After nearly 45 minutes I thought to myself I had better ask for Siri's help. By this time Siri let me know that I was nearly an hour away in the wrong direction. I was horrified! All I could think of was how late I would be, how much of the game I was missing and the look on my husband's face when I arrived. When I finally arrived, it was halftime and you guessed it, my husband asked, "where have you been?"

Too embarrassed to say I said, "I'll tell you about it later." Surely enough, I had missed the most amazing first half ever-gathering from what the parents shared with me. So, after the game, I apologized to my son and shared with the family what had happened. That night I learned a very valuable lesson. I learned that **although my pursuit was correct, the path to get me there was not.**

This reminds me of a scripture in Proverbs that says; there is a way that seems right to a man, but its end is the way of destruction.

Proverbs 14:12.

Thank God this was not a life or death situation, however, this situation opened my eyes to the need of not only remaining focused on the pursuit but on the correct path I am to take in order to get me to my destination.

EVERY RELATIONSHIP BEGINS WITH PURSUIT

Relationships are one of the most precious experiences God has given to us in this life. From our relationship with God, to husbands and wives, to mothers and daughters, even neighbors, friends and coworkers. Relationships are a necessary asset to our lives, but did you know that it takes pursuit to see any relationship flourish and grow? No relationship grows without a pursuit.

"Pursuit ignites passion, passion stirs desire, what you desire you go after and what you go after you stay in pursuit of."

When a man desires a woman, he goes after her. Single royal ladies! Lend me your ears.

NEVER LOWER THE STANDARD
for a man that's in pursuit of you. It's in his nature to go after what he desires, and he doesn't need your help by lowering the standard while he's in pursuit.

Men love the pursuit. Men love the challenge.

Men understand that if little effort is required then perhaps what they're pursuing is of little value.

Model yourself like Fort Knox, where because of the value, the contents are locked up tight! Remember, **ROYALTY ALWAYS COMES WITH A PRICE!** Therefore, don't lower the price. Keep the value high. Have you ever seen a Rolls-Royce discounted? They don't even ADVERTISE. However, the value of the car ALWAYS remains because the manufacturer understands the quality they have put into every automobile and the name has been established as **value**. Single ladies, this is how you are to think of yourself; Royal, unique, special, one of a kind and a value that is far above rubies. This is why we are to pursue God. Because when we pursue Him, He helps us to stay focused on the priority and reminds us of our value. I'm reminded of a parable that speaks about what the Kingdom of God is like and its value.

Matthew 13:45-46 NIV
[45] "Again, the kingdom of heaven is like a merchant looking for fine pearls. [46] When he found one of **great value**, he went away and sold everything he had and bought it.

When value is recognized there is no price a man or woman is not willing to pay.

Also, remember that

"Discounts attract bargain hunters not value seekers"

Just a little nugget to all of you single ladies of Royalty.

The Kingdom of God, which is God's way of doing things, is valuable to our lives. When you let go of your old mindsets, emotional patterns and fears of your past, you will see the abundance that has been awaiting you! There is abundance of love, freedom, healing, provision, peace, wealth, joy, wholeness. For the Kingdom of God provides abundance in areas money simply cannot buy. Therefore, Jesus accepted and paid the high ransom price in order to redeem us back to God. It is the will of God that none of us should perish or be separated eternally from Him, but to live with Him forever. The price of our separation from God was Calvary. Calvary is the price that had to be "PAID IN

FULL" in order for us to have access to all the benefits of the Kingdom. Now that you have access, don't stop there. Don't be like someone who comes to the front door and once the door is opened, they stand and marvel at the door. No, the King wants us to enter in and pursue Him, so that we may partake of all that's within the house. Let me encourage you. Become passionate in your pursuit of the King. Just like the Psalmist David said, "As the deer longs for the water so my soul longs after You O Lord!" Psalms 42:1

David was passionate about God's presence. He understood that, although he was a king, the crown meant nothing if he did not have the presence with him. He understood that everything he would need in order to lead the nation successfully was found in his pursuit of God's presence. David realized that

"Pursuit is pointless if passion is not present".

Passionate pursuit is what keeps us focused upon His will being fulfilled in our lives. The King does not want us to pursue Him out of duty but out of love. He wants us to desire being with Him. **He doesn't want us to seek Him for what's in His hand but for what's in His heart.** No one wants a person to be with them for their status, platform, money or connections. People long to have others around them who desire to be in their company for who they are not for what they have or what they can do. There's nothing more heartbreaking than when you discover that a close friend was only a Judas in disguise. This is why pursuit is necessary. Pursuit exposes the heart. It uncovers the reason why. Passionate pursuit will examine and expose whether your heart is truly after His. God is wise and knows that in order for you to obtain the crown, which is in His hand, you must be tested and proven in your pursuit for His heart. Yes, as you heed this wisdom, you must know this…. there will be test. This pursuit will be more about what you're willing to give up than what you're wanting to hold on to. Yet the pursuit is well worth it! In life, you will have choices. **Every choice has two things attached to it, reward or consequence**. Therefore, it is so important to make wise and calculated choices. No doubt, you will live out each choice, good and not so good. There is a royal crown that awaits you and the Lord is eagerly looking to see if you can carry the weight, beauty and responsibility that come with it.

Now I want to share something that many may not know. It may sound a little corny to you, but I enjoy watching the Miss America pageants. I like seeing the pomp and circumstance of it all. I enjoy the evening gowns, talent competition and the question/answer portion of the event. I find it so exciting as the final five become the final three and the final three become the final two. I think it's amazing that out of all 50 states, just two women are left to be selected as the winner. Both are talented, intelligent, beautiful, worthy of wearing the crown but only one will walk away with it. As the music plays, excitement builds in the audience. The reigning Miss America takes her last official walk before crowning the new Miss America. As the host builds excitement in the crowd, the two finalists huddle together in anticipation of hearing their name. Then the host announces the moment that we've all been waiting for. The years of practice, preparation, commitment and dedication all come down to this. Yet, as all of this is going on, there is one question that rings in my mind and I begin to consider **"Does she know the weight of the responsibility she's about to receive?"** Because up until this point everything has been in preparation for the crown, but now comes the time for one of them to receive the title and wear the crown. As exciting as this is, only one will receive the weight of responsibility. There will be expectations, responsibilities and constant scrutiny of how she manages this position. Though all 50 contestants were in pursuit only one will receive the crown.

Thank God we are not competing for ONE CROWN, but we are all pursuing a crown that the Lord has waiting for each of us.

2 Timothy 4:8 NIV
[8] Now there is in store for me the crown of righteousness, which the Lord, the righteous Judge, will award to me on that day---and not only to me, but also to all who have longed for his appearing.

Like any pageant there will be things we must do in order to prepare us for the crown. We must refine our skills, maintain a teachable spirit, build strong character, walk in the spirit and follow His instructions continuously. As you continue your pursuit after His heart, all that He has in his hand will be given to you. No matter what, keep pursuing the Lord. Ask yourself this question, "Is what I'm currently going after truly worth this pursuit? Is it leading me closer to the heart of God and His Kingdom, or is it leading me further away?" Remember, the Lord finds no pleasure when you draw back in your passionate pursuit of Him. Let's look at some things we must do in order to prepare us for this responsibility.

CHAPTER 3

THE CROWN OF RESPONSIBILITY

Arise! For the matter is your responsibility....We are also with you so be of good courage. (Ezra 10:4)

When you hear the word, "responsibility", what thoughts come to mind? Work? Care? It's all on your shoulders? It's yours to succeed or fail? I believe that it's thoughts such as these which cause most people to be frightened of the very mention of the word **responsibility**. Many thoughts swirl in your mind with the fear of "what could happen if I fail." This thought is commonly more than most are willing to deal with. Every leader, to include those within our homes, our government and those we admire on television, have been given the opportunity to impact lives and direct the course of change within their communities, their nation and the world around them.

Responsibility is a built-in component for all who have been given a gift, a voice, a platform and an opportunity to speak into the lives of others. You must always remember that you are an example, a model. You are to show and demonstrate the authentic leadership that is necessary for today's generation.

The current generation is raising her voice with cries for change. They are looking for leaders who are willing to abandon their comfort and push aside their prestige.

"Greatness will never be found in normalcy but in great Responsibility!"

The greatest book ever written makes this statement; "Let he who has an ear hear". I want to ask you this question, "CAN YOU HEAR?" Can you hear the sound of multitudes of women, wives, mothers and daughters calling out and asking

"WHO WILL SHOW US, WHO WILL TRAIN US AND WHO WILL TEACH US?"

Who will model what true Responsibility looks like?

As women, wives and mothers, we have a tremendous responsibility afforded unto us. We have an urgency to impart into the hearts, minds and souls of women and especially this generation. We must impart a true and authentic understanding of KINGDOM ROYALTY and we must be willing to make the pursuit.

It's becoming increasingly difficult today to identify those willing to assume responsibility. In fact, many are choosing to defer responsibility to the next generation. It's becoming increasingly common for individuals to defer the responsibility for their actions, attitudes, families, marriages, community upon someone else or something else. This disbursement of responsibility is as old as Adam and Eve. As we read here in Genesis 3:9-13 we will see how Adam and his wife responded when faced with the question of responsibility.

Genesis 3:9-13 NIV
[9] But the Lord God called to the man, "Where are you?" [10] He answered, "I heard you in the garden, and I was afraid because I was naked; so, I hid." [11] And HE said, "Who told you that you were naked? Have you eaten from the tree that I commanded you not to eat from?" [12] The man said, "The woman you put here with me-she gave me some fruit from the tree, and I ate it." [13] Then the Lord God said to the woman, "What is this you have done?" The woman said, "The serpent deceived me, and I ate."

After reading these verses, I found it interesting, that God asked different questions to each of them. Within these questions lie the significance of their responsibility. In Genesis 3:9, the Lord God asked Adam **"WHERE ARE YOU?"** Yet, in Genesis 3:13 the Lord asked Eve **"WHAT HAVE YOU DONE?"** To each of them I believe the questions were appropriately asked. To Eve, the Lord asked, "What have you done?" Not just to correct her, but to bring Eve to a recognition and understanding of something more powerful than even she was aware of. This was not just concerning her action in giving Adam the fruit but "WHAT" she used in order to convince Adam to take of the fruit, which he was instructed by God, not to do. Do you know what it is? It's called **INFLUENCE**.

Now to Adam, the Lord asked "WHERE ARE YOU?" not because He didn't know Adam's location but to signify to Adam what he lost, which was his **POSITION.**

Adam was given position and he was placed in the garden first to carry out the likeness of God in the earth. What Adam failed to understand was that position has with it rights, privileges and responsibilities. Let's look at the word position. According to Webster's Dictionary; the word **Position** is defined as being first, to lead, to be in charge, given in Position. Position was given to the male first. He was to manage the garden, manage all within the garden, manage his position and protect it. Position, by right of definition, requires decision making, management, oversight and protection of all that is under the care of that position. Adam had something to be responsible for and that something is called

POSITION. Position carries within its definition order, rank, management and responsibility. Therefore, God's original intent for Adam was for him to manage, care for and protect what he had been given which was **POSITION**. The responsibility of his position was to manage the garden with great care, to protect and develop all that was within the garden to include the precious gift, given to him in the garden, named Eve. She, like Adam, was also given an area of responsibility. Something for her to give great care to. A responsibility given to her so soft yet oh so strong, that which could be evidently seen yet delicately hidden. Something so powerful that kings and leaders in great positions seek after it. For without it, they know they can do very little to nothing at all. Without it, their voice becomes a faint whisper in the forest and merely another number among the crowd. Can you guess what this powerful responsibility is? It's called **INFLUENCE**. Influence is so powerful that **POSITION** will yield to its gentle request. An individual who possesses **INFLUENCE** can achieve so much more than a person merely in a position, because it yields the power to redirect the hearts and minds of those in a position to fulfill their desires. You may question how is that? Allow me to explain it this way. Have you ever gone shopping with a friend looking for that special outfit and after trying on several you find one you love only to have your friend give you a look that makes you reconsider your decision? The outfit is beautiful. It fits well, you love the color, you're paying for it but her look causes you to reconsider buying it. That is how influence works. Her influence and the value of her opinion caused you to redirect your decision. Get the picture? Influence is a great strength in the heart of a woman submitted to God, but it can be very dangerous in the heart of an immature or insecure woman who uses it to manipulate others into satisfying her own desires. Remember **POSITION HAS POWER BUT INFLUENCE HAS GREAT STRENGTH**. *Therefore, influence must be managed (controlled).* Influence, absent of knowing its responsibility, can be disastrous to a people, a family, a church and a society. Be discerning of those who influence your thinking away from what or who you have been assigned to. For

"whenever you have been negatively influenced against someone who has been assigned to help you, you become the loser".

The enemy did this with Eve. He played with Eve's mind by twisting God's word causing Eve to abuse her influence thus enabling him to gain what he wanted all along; Adam's position of dominion. The enemy wasn't after Eve as much as he was after Adam's POSITION. However, he realized that in order to take the position from Adam, he needed the strength of influence possessed by Eve. We will learn more about Position and Influence in chapter 5. Until then let's discuss the whole idea of responsibility in the next chapter.

CHAPTER 4

Responsibility; God's Idea

Responsibility is at it's best when we all take our part in it.

~ *Dr. DeNae LeMay*

I think it would be beneficial for us to begin this chapter by defining RESPONSIBILITY;

-IN HEBREW, responsibility is defined as a burden... meaning you may not always enjoy it, but you are committed to it! IN THE GREEK responsibility means to be placed over something. Webster defines responsibility as being totally dependable, you could also say it this way, (RE-SPONSE-ABLE) or **able to respond** to matters with a correct response, to be accountable for something within one's power or control.

Responsibility has been in the mind of God since the beginning. God gave Adam and Eve three major areas in which to govern and have responsibility over. The first area is;

DOMINION RESPONSIBILITY-
They were responsible to exercise dominion in the earth. According to Genesis 1:26 it says, **"Let THEM have Dominion"** Here the Lord is stating that the two creations called Adam and Eve, will have as a part of their mandate, the ability to have dominion. They were given rule and full access to all the territory on the earth. They were to rule over the birds, the fish, the cattle and the creeping things and over all the earth. Isn't that great to know? We were not given authority to rule over people but over all the earth. We were not created to be subjects but to rule the earth and thereby making it subject to us. Isn't that powerful to know? That we have been given dominion responsibility? Pardon me for a moment but I just think that is absolutely powerful!

INCREASE RESPONSIBILITY-

We are responsible to re-produce and increase in the earth. According to Genesis 1:28 which says; Let THEM be fruitful and multiply. This is a verse that so many think of "only" in respect to having children. Yet, I would like to add that our responsibility for increasing in the earth does not stop there. For we not only are to increase mankind in the earth, but we are to fulfill the will of God by increasing His likeness, culture and the environment of Heaven in the earth. For **earth was literally created to be a COLONY** (a distant land established in a foreign territory to represent the home country) of Heaven. The earth has so much increase within it that we should lack no good thing! Not only are we called to multiply humans, but we should multiply the integrity, character, nature and the very heart of God. We do that by bringing light wherever we go and within every sphere of influence we enter. We are increase conduits! We increase businesses, companies, communities, families and cultures with the principles of the King. *Financially we are carriers of increase and streams of revenue.* Remember, it's the Lord who gives you the power to get wealth (Deuteronomy 8:18). **Your wealth is not limited to the company**

that employed you, nor the customers who purchase from you, but your capacity is unlimited according to the "POWER" He has placed into your hands! What is "The Gift" God has given you? That special anointing that you were born to serve the world? Your gift will bring you great wealth and place you before great people (Proverbs 18:16).

Do you bake well, sew well… how about serve well? Guess what? That's where your "wealth transfer" will come from. **The great wealth transfer is underway,** but it will not just fall out of the sky nor be received the way the children of Israel received manna when they left Egypt. *Your wealth will be transferred as you provide solutions, solve problems, serve your gifts and talents to the world.* I could go on about that, but I'll save it for a future book.

EARTH RESPONSIBILITY
We are responsible to care for the earth and all that is within the earth. According to (Genesis 1:28) it reads; "Let THEM fill and subdue the earth". **It's our responsibility to take the**

power of the word, speak to the natural areas and expect the earth to respond. By faith, we are His representative in the earth. Therefore, we have the same ability to speak to creation and by faith command His will to be manifested. That's why Jesus could speak to the wind and the waves and command them to obey. (Luke 8:22-25). That's how Jesus could speak to the fig tree and command it to wither. (Mark 11:12-25). That's how the prophet spoke to the sun and commanded it to stand still at Gideon in order for him to win the battle. That's how Elijah commanded the clouds to cease from releasing rain for a season of time and it had to obey him (1 King 17-18). They were walking in their EARTH RESPONSIBILITY. THAT'S SIMPLY AWESOME TO KNOW!

Adam was given responsibility to name all the animals and to care for the garden. He was also given responsibility to care for Eve and not to eat the fruit! As royalty, we should be aware that to whom much is given much will be required. It's not a word that we should run from but an opportunity we must learn to embrace. God has given you everything you need to walk it out and to succeed. Yet, like Queen Esther you must recognize that **you have been chosen for such a time as this**.

CHAPTER 5

POSITION AND INFLUENCE

"Responsibility is weighty, but obedience will lighten the load."
Dr. DeNae LeMay

Now, as we relink, let's look at a verse of scripture that will help open our eyes to this revelation discussed in chapter 3.
Let's read Genesis 1:28 NKJV to understand where this all began.

[28] Then God blessed them, and God said to them, "Be fruitful and multiply; fill the earth and subdue it; have dominion over the fish of the sea, over the birds of the air, and over every living thing that moves on the earth."

Adam was given **POSITION** as his place to fulfill the mandated assignment of **DOMINION.** The woman Eve was given **INFLUENCE** as her place to fulfill the

DOMINION mandate assignment in the earth. Adam and Eve **BOTH carry gifts**, yet each one operates stronger from their respective, God-given place of responsibility.

God, in His amazing wisdom, created Adam and Eve physically different but spiritually the same.

Both were created to lead and both were given rights and privileges to exercise dominion over the earth. According to Genesis 1:26, we learn that this was their purpose. However, In order to accomplish the Dominion mandate, they will need the support of each other's God-given strength. When you hear the word **DOMINION** do you think of weakness or strength? If you said strength, you are correct! As in Monopoly, you now get to move past go. Allow me to share an example of this with you. I have a tremendous family. I have a wonderful husband (Stacy), three amazing sons (Christian, Uriah, and Benjamin) and my one beautiful daughter (Jasmine). We've moved a few times and with a family this size we have chosen to move most of our items ourselves. (We moved so many times we almost started a moving company. Lol.)

Because we have an even number within our household (6), we always paired up the children so that the weight of the item was compatible to the strength of the children.

In other words, they were a well-balanced team and we never paired a weaker with a stronger. Both children had to be fully capable to lift the item equally. That's the picture of the male and female creation. Though physically different, they are equal in their ability to carry the item called DOMINION in the earth! Whenever you lift something weighty, you need someone equally as strong to assist. That's why women are called "help meets" because when he operates from his strength called **POSITION** and she operates from her strength called **INFLUENCE**, there's nothing they cannot accomplish together! *God paired Adam together with the most qualified complement for his assignment.* That's right, Eve was one who could "Hold her own" weight in the Dominion mandate and both were given this charge that THEY may rule TOGETHER.
"LET THEM HAVE DOMINION".
Had these two gifts been properly used TOGETHER, they (Adam and Eve) would

have been unstoppable. That's why the enemy devised his plan to sabotage God's plan for man on the earth. However, the mandate given to them must still be fulfilled! We must not consider that because ADAM and EVE RELINQUISHED their responsibility, we cannot fulfill the Dominion Mandate. We must continue to *Pursue* what has been decreed and established as the King's rule in our lives. What wasn't realized in the Garden is that these two powerful gifts carry a great weight of responsibility and they must be managed under God's authority.

The **four main components of responsibility** are these:

VALUE
PURPOSE
REWARDS
CONSEQUENCES
Let's take a closer look into each of these areas.

VALUE
- ## <u>Responsibility has Value</u>

When we consider the word value, we think of words such as **worth, importance and usefulness**. In describing responsibility, I believe these three words encompass the meaning with great accuracy. I ask you this question, when companies are looking to hire managers and other up line positions, how valuable in their search do you believe they prioritize the quality of responsibility? I think it would be pretty high, wouldn't you say? To identify qualified applicants is one thing but to hire qualified and RESPONSIBLE applicants is something totally different. Responsibility is not just showing up on time and doing the assignment, even though that is important. However, having a person of excellence who understands responsibility is what every employer is looking for!

My husband is an entrepreneur at heart. He loves business and is extremely anointed in this area. In fact, one might call him a "serial entrepreneur." It has always been his dream to not only own his own business but to have several streams that would be used as a conduit to bless others. As business owners, responsibility is what we are constantly mindful of. Yet, locating others who will take the same level of care and responsibility for the business is challenging to say the least. In every business, stepping up to the plate of responsibility within the company is the difference-maker, it is the game-changing move that will win you the leading positions and cause you to climb the ladder in record time. Thereby, bringing exponential wealth into your hands. You are not just paid to work! There are many people who can do that. You're not paid just to show up, but you are paid to solve problems, to find and provide solutions! Your true value is found in being "RESPONSE-ABLE" and to solve problems to difficult situations, crises and challenges. So, the next time you are given the opportunity to solve a difficult challenge in your company and you shy away from providing a solution, just remember that your value has just been identified!

PURPOSE

- ## **Responsibility has Purpose**

Everything God created was created for a purpose

Your eyes were created for a purpose and that purpose was sight. Your hands were created for a purpose and that purpose is to serve, build and create. The hairs on your head, the fish in the sea, the birds and even the trees were all created for a purpose. Purpose gives meaning and understanding to everything in life and without understanding purpose (the why), abuse becomes the result. For the purpose of all creation is found in its design. That's why it is paramount for believers to know their purpose and accept their responsibility. Our King has entrusted the mandate of earth's Dominion into your care. However, if you pass off that responsibility or dismiss it all together, then when the outcome does not match your desire, you have no one to blame but yourself. Whether you are a teacher, mother, singer, CEO or pastor, every position is important in fulfilling His plan in the earth.

REWARDS

- ## <u>Responsibility has Rewards</u>

Everyone loves rewards. *Rewards are used as incentives and encouragement to continue.*

This is why stores love issuing reward cards. They know that if they reward you for each purchase, you'll not only come back for more, but you will tell others to do the same. When rewards and benefits are received, they strengthen you with encouragement and they motivate you to fulfill the assignment. When we read the account of David, the young Shepherd boy who went off to obtain a report for his father concerning how his older brothers were doing in battle, David observed an opportunity to demonstrate responsibility. On this day,... he would not pass it up.
Let's read the account.

1Samuel 17:20-26

20 Early in the morning David left the flock in the care of a shepherd, loaded up and set out, as Jesse had directed. He reached the camp as the army was going out to its battle positions, shouting the war cry. 21 Israel and the Philistines were drawing up their lines facing each other. 22 David left his things with the keeper of supplies, ran to the battle lines and asked his brothers how they were. 23 As he was talking with them, Goliath, the Philistine champion from Gath, stepped out from his lines and shouted his usual defiance, and David heard it. 24 Whenever the Israelites saw the man, they all fled from him in great fear.

25 Now the Israelites had been saying, "Do you see how this man keeps coming out? He comes out to defy Israel. The king will give great wealth to the man who kills him. He will also give him his daughter in marriage and will exempt his family from taxes in Israel."

[26] David asked the men standing near him, **"What will be done for the man who kills this Philistine and removes this disgrace from Israel?** Who is this uncircumcised Philistine that he should defy the armies of the living God?"

David accepted the challenge, but he also inquired **"what will be done for the man that kills this Philistine?"** In other words **"What's the reward"?** David took responsibility to confront this enemy who was found mocking the people and defying his God. Yet he also inquired about the reward. I love it! Not only did he defeat this so-called undefeated champion called Goliath, but he received great reward because he took responsibility and said, "bring it on!" my God is with me and as He was with me when I fought the lion and the bear so shall He be with me in this fight!"
Don't run from responsibility. In doing so, you may be running from your greatest reward!

CONSEQUENCES

- ## **<u>Responsibility has Consequences</u>**

This is probably one of the most difficult areas of discussion. When we look at our families, communities, schools, media and government, we see the constant passing of responsibility and the effects that it has unleashed. Yet we should applaud the many men and women who are willing to be stable pillars of character and integrity for this generation. These are our true heroes! Individuals who will stand in the way of complete implosion within our families and society. For without them, the consequences would be devastating.

"Consequences are never experienced without a cause."

Transformational thinking is of the highest priority in order to witness the correct responses in our lives and our society. When we assume responsibility, we exhibit the fullness of true leadership. How is it that those who are called leaders, willingly accept the praises for greatness but do not accept the responsibility for defeats? As parents, we have responsibility for our children in their young formative years. We care for what they see, what they hear, where they go, what they do and what we expose them to. Yet, when they become of age, they become responsible for their own decisions, choices and outcomes. Even with this realization, many parents continue far past the age of accountability, making decisions for their children, alleviating responsibility and delaying the maturation process while calling it love. Instead of doing the hard, tough job by allowing them to develop through incremental decision-making opportunities, they wait until they are of college age or even older. Then they criticize the child's decisions, leaving them broken, crippled and inadequate to manage their now adult life. If this is something you have walked through or something your experiencing now don't beat yourself up about it. Do what God gives us the beauty of doing, repent and correct it. Make the needed adjustments today. If this is your story go to your child and repent. Locate the root of "why" this was allowed and help them through the process of recovery.

Do not do the process for them! Don't cripple them any longer! But instead strengthen them to be the leaders they have been called to be.

There are many who pass off responsibility as if it was yesterday's passing fashion, not fully understanding the consequences of doing so. When responsibility is not taken it leaves tumultuous voids. My Spiritual Father, Dr Myles Munroe once said; "Where purpose is not known abuse is inevitable"!!
What a powerful and true statement indeed.
Just ask ADAM AND EVE!

CHAPTER 6
THE BEAUTY OF
THE CROWN- INFLUENCE

"Influence is so powerful, God had to place it under position."
Dr DeNae LeMay

I made the above statement earlier, but I believe it bears repeating. The necessity to remember this is vital. Women, we must not use what was given to us for expanding the Kingdom as a tool to manipulate, maneuvering things and people to favor our own desires. Instead, we must use this gift for impacting the earth for the Kings purpose. Eve was entrusted with a very powerful gift and responsibility. She was given the responsibility of influence, which was to be used for the mandate of Dominion. Let's look at this scripture.

(Genesis 3:6 MEV)
"When the woman saw that the tree was good for food, that it was pleasing to the eyes and a tree desirable to make one wise, she took of its fruit and ate; and she gave to her husband with her, and he ate."

Influence has tremendous consequences attached to it. When influence is managed well it can change, redirect, reposition, resolve and reconcile people. Yet, if it's managed poorly, it can do major and extensive damage. I believe THAT IS WHY GOD ASKED EVE "WHAT HAVE YOU DONE?" Our Creator knows what He created, and He knows just how powerful and persuasive influence can be. Daily, the Lord invested consistent time with Adam in the cool of the day, imparting, teaching, sharing, and revealing Himself to Adam. **Position was given to Adam to model before Eve.** Adam was responsible to impart into Eve the information he heard from God in the cool of the day.

I am going to make a statement that I want you to share with your husbands and husbands to be. Trust me! What I am about to share will be a game changer for your marriage. When he understands this statement, it will make a huge difference in your relationship. Are you ready? Here it is; **Husbands, do not leave your wives empty of your impartation! Your words release value and if you leave her empty, she will find someone or something to fill that need!** Adam should have replicated the leadership model demonstrated before him. Adam was responsible to lead the one formed and fashioned as the perfect complement for him. He was to lead so that the destiny upon their lives would be fulfilled. Yet instead, he yielded to Eve and her influence for the word said that "she turned and gave to him and he DID eat!" How is it that the one positioned to lead becomes the follower?

Influence is like a gift. This gift was given to the female as their strength in order to carry out the dominion mandate. Influence is necessary for those who are called "help meet". Understand this, in order for POSITION (which is what was given to the male) to be effective in the earth for dominion, the "helper" he needed had to be given a strength equal in power to his position.

This equal strength would bring balance and give each of them their gifted area to rule from. When they operate in order, in submission and honor of the strength given to each of them, they would surely achieve DOMINION. Women of Royalty, you were given the power of influence. Influence has great ability and we must be responsible with it. **Influence has gentle, yet convincing strength, while Position Possesses Power and Dominating Love**. I believe that is why the Bible gives this instruction to husbands "Husbands love your wives." For if women are void of what they need (love), they will function from a place of brokenness and emptiness leading them to mismanage their gift in order to fulfill that need. This operation of the mismanaged gift is known as manipulation! And oh, how dangerous it is for an influencer to influence you from a place of manipulation and not from love (Agape). I have another word for husbands. Husbands, if you are detecting this in your wife, check to see how you are loving her? Fathers observe your daughters and brothers cover your sisters. **The office of Position must always cover and manage the VALUE of influence.** Influence carries such a great responsibility that if left uncovered, it has the ability to short-circuit and even delay heavens plans for man on the earth. **Influence is precious, powerful and valuable, therefore it must be COVERED and PROTECTED.**

Influence is defined as the capacity to influence the character, behavior or development of someone or something. Influence is also the ability to affect or change someone's thoughts, actions or behavior. That's why unbeknownst to Eve, the adversary who came dressed in a serpent's attire, desired Adam's position and understood that the most effective way to gain this position was through Eve's influence. The enemy contrived a scheme which was clever, yet powerful enough and legally correct, to win himself all the rights, privileges and benefits that belonged to Adam. The adversary understood that in order for him to gain position he must obtain it through the means of influence. Trust me when I say this, Influence is POWERFUL!
Responsibility is what Eve was given to manage in the form of influence and she yielded her responsibility to something that

proved to be even stronger than both position and influence. Can you imagine what that was? ...That was **HUMAN DESIRE**. I know we're going deep here, but let's see just how this works.

(Genesis 3:6) reads "when the woman SAW that the tree was good for food, that it was PLEASING TO THE EYES and a tree "DESIRABLE" to make one wise, she took of its fruit and ate; and she GAVE to her husband with her, and HE ATE.

Did you see the process! The **first thing DESIRE does is attract your attention**. It does that to awaken in you a taste for something you were not aware of. DESIRE then speaks to your senses (taste, touch, sight, smell, and hearing) to inform you of the activity's pleasure but not its consequences. After desire has attached itself to influence, (for the intended purpose of affecting and or changing someone's thoughts, actions or behavior) the process/plan has now begun. All that remains now is for POSITION to vacate, leaving the adversary free reign to take ownership of what has been abandoned, which was Adam's position.

After willingly submitting his position to her influence, Adam gave the enemy legal access and authority over the earth and all of Creation. Since this time all of Creation has been awaiting the manifested return of the original sons of God. (Rom 8:19)

Let me give you an example of this. King Saul was given the responsibility to lead God's people and to heed the voice of God through the prophet Samuel. King Saul was also given the command by God to destroy ALL the Amalekites, yet he heeded the voice and opinions of the people. King Saul allowed the voice of the people to INFLUENCE his decision to disobey the full counsel of God's command. Given Saul's decision to consider and reason over obeying God's command, Saul had to be removed from his POSITION of responsibility. Once again, we see Position succumb to Influence. I'm sure that if King Saul knew the weight of the consequences, he was about to encounter from what seemed to be a simple adjustment to God's instructions, he would have chosen differently. If only he could have understood what was at stake and foreseen the consequences that would follow his poor judgment and insecure decision.

Saul mistakenly forgot that his crown carried more than his name but the name of the Lord, creator of Heaven and earth. God is very serious about what He gives us responsibility to do. Therefore, I suggest that we also take our responsibility just as seriously before we find that our crown has been removed and we, like Saul, find no place for repentance. Selah!

If only Adam and Eve had understood that they were the son and daughter of the creator King! If only Eve had understood that she was created to be the royal influence to all of mankind. What if Eve had understood that she was created to live and reign as royalty? Do you think the enemy would have been able to manipulate her? Thereby controlling her influence?

I know this has been a rather eye-opening chapter. I trust that it has caused you to press deeper in your understanding, to comprehend the awesome privilege and responsibility we have in wearing the crown. I'm not sure if you think like me, but I prefer having as much information available so that I can be fully aware of what's required from me. My desire is to equip you in such a way that you also may not become double-minded in your royal pursuit. With that said, lets proceed to the next chapter and dig even deeper.

CHAPTER 7

ROYALTY REQUIRES

When you understand what is expected, it removes all the excuses.

~ *Dr. DeNae LeMay*

Do you recall the story I shared with you about Queen Victoria? Well, just like the queen, you are in line for greatness! I want to remind you that there are amazing promises awaiting you. This is not charismatic encouragement but a true fact. You are a descendant of Royalty and you have been pre-destined with a great inheritance. It's important that you refuse to squander opportunities presented to you by the King.

Whenever opportunities are not utilized, it positions us to lose time, purpose and destiny.

When I began my pursuit, there was a realization of certain areas in my life that **required me to make immense adjustments and changes.** From the inside out, I knew this metamorphosis was necessary. Unlike the change that happens without your consent or knowledge, I was fully aware it would require my willingness throughout the process. Every caterpillar goes through a process in order to become the beautiful butterfly that captivates us as it flutters through the air during the springtime. This is the value of pursuit. Royal Pursuit reveals weak areas that you were not aware of, Areas that need adjustments and refinement in order to reinforce strength in that area. Two things I have learned over the years

1. The more you go after the King, the more you desire to become like Him.

2. The more you go after The King, the more He will require of you.

That's why the Lord said, "My ways are not your ways and My thoughts are not your thoughts" (Isa.55:8).

In this Chapter, I would like to share **8 areas you will encounter along your Pursuit of the crown.** These areas will require change in order to advance and achieve.

1. ROYALTY REQUIRES TRAINING

Training is necessary and should be a welcomed discipline in our lives. We all need training and therefore need a quality Trainer. We must be trained in order to remove the old mind which is set after the world's patterns, beliefs and ideas.

(Romans 12:2 NLT) says, *"Don't copy the behavior and customs of this world, but let God transform you into a new person by changing the way you think. Then you will learn to know God's will for you, which is good and pleasing and perfect."* NLT

Having a teachable heart is necessary in order to be trained. As you allow the Holy Spirit, who is your teacher and tutor to train you, the Holy Spirit helps prepare you for each assignment. Like Queen Victoria, I wonder if you knew what was ahead, would your response to the teaching, training, testing and refining you must go through simply be "I'LL BE GOOD?" Would it be "I won't complain," Would it be "I won't quit," Would it be " I won't charge God foolishly." Would it be, Yes… "God, I'll be good". How you think through the process of training is vitally important. For as a man thinks in his heart so is he (Proverbs 23:7). Thinking is a practice which requires consistency and training. **You must be taught not "what" to think but "how" to properly think** and how to think wisely as a Royal Ambassador.

Here are some questions to ask yourself; What are you meditating on? How well are you hearing God's voice? What do you think of constantly? What is the source and motivation of your thoughts? So much of who and what you are is birthed from your thought life. We have been trained for years to develop thought patterns established from this world's system, yet we are not of this world nor this system.

John 17:16 "You are in the world but not of this world". Your thinking should reflect the culture and origin of your country. You are a Kingdom citizen and a royal Priesthood, a peculiar people, His own Special People. You may appear like them physically, but you are not of them. That's why thinking requires training and training produces growth. Even Jesus grew. He grew in stature and wisdom according to Luke 2:52.

I believe that Jesus grew in favor with God and man because He was submitted to the process of being trained. The bible says that even Jesus learned obedience Hebrews 5:8

Training causes growth and growth causes increase. Did you know that when all children of royalty are born, a tutor is assigned to assist them in their process of maturation? The tutor is assigned to prepare them for royalty and for royal responsibility. The same is given for the woman of royalty. You were given the Holy Spirit to be your tutor/teacher. He will guide you into all that you must know as you Pursue the Crown.

In John 14:26 Jesus said; "But the Counselor, the Holy Spirit whom the Father will send in my name, will teach you all that I taught you." Your Heavenly Father thought of everything you would need and made provision so that you would lack nothing. He made sure that you would mature into the full measure of who and what He intended for you to become. **Royal training is vital and who you receive it from is critical. Beware of unqualified tutors!** They may appear correct, but their teachings are void and incorrect. *We have many teachers today but not many tutors* (mentors). *Teachers may tell you how but True tutors* (mentors) will SHOW YOU HOW.

2. ROYALTY REQUIRES DEVELOPMENT

Royal development is necessary for Royal deployment
  ~ Dr Stacy LeMay

When you think of the word "development" do you think of words like "stages, process and time?"
Development, *by definition, is the process of growth.* In order for you to be properly prepared for responsibility you must go through a process and embrace development.

Like a person who exercises in order to build muscle, they must go through a process of development.

Things today have advanced so rapidly that it may be difficult to recall items which took time to develop, such as a photo. You see, back in my day, about 1,000 years ago lol, we took photos not by cell phone but on a separate device called a camera. Some cameras were small enough to carry around your neck or in your purse. Each camera had a compartment where film was to be placed. Once the roll of film was used up we would take the film out of the camera and deliver it to a place for processing also known as **developing**. It could take days or hours, depending on the number of photos taken and the amount of money you wanted to spend for expedited **processing**. Once the film was dropped off, it was then sent to a film developing room for processing. This was where the film would be separated from its case and placed carefully into a solution which would take seemingly blank, underdeveloped film and in the process of time, you would see the images develop right before your eyes. What was once a process is now a thing of the past. Within a few seconds you have a beautiful photo and can save it for as long as you like on your personal mobile device or in the cloud. I really enjoy these modern conveniences, but I am reminded that God's methods are still His methods and He still believes in **process and development**. You must be developed in communication, in confidence, in who you are and whose you are. You may need development as a mother, wife, business woman, friend or minister. Development takes time and patience. Don't become frustrated if you don't see results right away. Perhaps you need a mentor to help you develop properly through the process. **A mentor is someone who will walk alongside you in order to help you see areas in your life that you do not and push you to become what you never thought possible.** I happen to know of a great one (smile). If you are ready to commit to the process, then visit my webpage @www.Developingqueens.com for more information.

Keep your eyes on your lane.

Watching the development path of others, is the fastest way to become discouraged and quit the process.

"You won't be rewarded for how well you WATCHED their race but how well you RAN yours!"

The plan He has for your life is so BIG that it is mandatory that you be developed by a mature mentor. You must be developed in mind soul and body because when you arrive after your process, nothing will be able to disqualify you from receiving your crown.

3. ROYALITY REQUIRES THE RIGHT ATTITUDE

An Attitude is not something you are born with. Instead they are developed over time.
  ~ Dr DeNae LeMay

Those who are of Royalty carry themselves with an attitude of dignity, honor, strength, steadfastness, confidence and a positive outlook. Just like the three Hebrew boys when they spoke to King Nebuchadnezzar and declared "Our God is able". They didn't respond with a defeated mentality but with a can-do mentality. They didn't respond with a fearful attitude but with a fearless attitude. Why? Because they believed in the strength of their God. **Even in the face of their most challenging moment they had a lion - like attitude.**

That attitude was one of strength, resolve, assurance, and victory. As royalty, leadership is in your spiritual DNA. It's your responsibility to lead and not retreat. To stand up and not cower down. It's your responsibility to go if no one else will and to do great things even if no one else does. That's the attitude of royalty. You carry an attitude of compassion and love just as your King does. You should be mindful of **how you speak**, **what you say** and always keep in mind that **the tone you use to present your message will often produce the response you desire.** Being royal doesn't mean you have to be mean and being kind doesn't mean that you are soft. *Learn the attitudes of royalty and you will see doors open wide to accommodate your arrival!*

4. ROYALTY REQUIRES CHARACTER

NO TRUE PUBLIC FIGURE HAS A PERSONAL LIFE!
~ Dr Myles Munroe

"Character" is a word we hear often and yet I believe it has not been explored deeply enough. My Spiritual Father, the late Dr Myles Munroe, taught that

"Character is an internal governing more than it is an external governing."
~ Dr. Myles Munroe

Let me explain. The Bible says in (1 Corinthians 11:31) ESV "But if we judged ourselves truly, we would not be judged". In other words, if we would take the word of God and use it (as our standard) to govern our own lives, then we would not have a need for others to judge us. It's like driving on a highway. If we would obey speed limits we would not need the police to judge us as law breakers (by writing us a ticket), because we would exercise self- government versus external government.
Internal self-government automatically deals with our external behavior, such as our

thoughts, our conversations, our personal responses which make up our character. *Character is who you are at ALL times.* **Character development will reduce the need for costly experiential development.** Many live from experience to experience never learning from the previous experiences but instead adding to them. This is how some women have set their minds and subsequently struggle with God's love because they believe He's unloving, unkind and ultimately punishing them. What they are doing is simply repeating cycles and are unable to see the consequences that are built into their choices. **Consequences are not designed to destroy you or break your spirit, but are designed to help correct wrong behavior and develop character.** *The Father's intention is not to break you but to build you.* To build sustainable character in you.

That's why (Proverbs 3:12) says "whom the Lord loves he corrects even as a father the son in whom he delights." KJV

As you develop in character you will also develop in loyalty, honesty, patience, integrity, purity, forgiveness and obedience. **Character**

is also being unmovable and fixed in your belief. That's why even if someone mis-treats you, your character, which is based on the word of God, does not change. I know this is a difficult one, but *if you deny your flesh and allow the word to work, you will become like the Statue of Liberty in New York City, unmovable.* No matter what, choose to exercise forgiveness, grow in love and watch what's released from your obedience. This is why you build your life on character, not on convenience.

5. ROYALTY REQUIRES ROYAL BEHAVIOR

I'd like to be known as the Queen of people's hearts
-Princess Diana

This is a powerful statement from the late Princess Diana. Her fame exceeded far beyond Buckingham Palace largely due to her heart of compassion for all mankind. She fulfilled this desire and became queen in the hearts of people worldwide. Her service spoke volumes above the words used against her. She was a game-changer within the royal family.

As royalty, many may not understand why you behave the way you do. They may not understand that the behavior of a person will determine the direction of their lives. *If you observe royalty closely, you will notice that they are not given over to excessive communication.* They communicate what is important and what must be said. Their words have so much weight and value that, based upon the question, they may or may not even respond. In fact, sometimes no response is the response. Royalty doesn't just answer flipidly. Those of Royalty make it a practice to give careful thought to matters presented to them, knowing that having a correct outcome is imperative. That's why you will not hear those who understand their royalty speaking unproductive, profane words. *They understand the power of their words and refuse to curse their future over a temporary moment.* They don't curse the people they have been sent to serve. Unfortunately, today's women, who were created as royalty, will curse their husband, children, business and church. This is their way of "keeping it real" as they call it. However, true royalty understands the value of what they say. True royalty will cease being wasteful with their words and will always remember that it's not about them, but about the ones they have been sent to serve.

How you behave publicly and privately is crucial to your assignment. Can you imagine owning a company and sending representatives with hopes of expanding your company, only to discover that your representatives were rude, inattentive and demanding towards those they were sent to serve?
Would you give them a pass and brush it off as just a bad day or would you require a different behavior from them? If you want to stay in business, I would hope you chose the latter. God is looking to you to be His representative in the earth. How you do that is always important to Him. How you give, love, serve, behave and communicate with others, in and out of their presence, matters to Him. You will be the model and example to many. This is why development in this area is so important. Everything you have been given responsibility over is depending upon you. *It's important that you learn how to speak properly, remain calm, poised and confident.* Remember, your family and coworkers, whom you hope to influence, are

watching closely how you handle difficult situations.

Ask yourself these questions; How do I handle disappointments? How do I handle unexpected news? How do I handle rejection, betrayal, physical challenge? Remember, they are watching and looking for the leader in you to lead them through dark days. Your words have power and carry authority. When the Queen of England speaks, she does not fear if what she says will be carried out, because she has the power to change things and the Authority to make sure it gets done! **Authority will eat Power for lunch on any day of the week.** Authority can rewrite laws, reposition leaders, and shift you from one level to another dimension in one stroke of a pen. Joseph arose from the prison to the palace. Esther arose from being an orphan to being a Queen. David arose from shepherd boy to giant slayer in one day! Although it may have seemed sudden to many, their rise to prominence was being developed in "unseen" places for a very long time. Their development was preparing them for their one moment before the King. *Watch how you behave during your season of being* *overlooked.* Always remember that **"what man ignores the Lord will wake up, raise up, and set up for greatness!"**

6. ROYALTY REQUIRES CHANGE

There is nothing permanent except change
- *Heraclitus*

The most consistent thing in life is change and change is what happens to us all. Change allows children to grow and mature into adults. **Change has brought us from pony express to private jets**. Without change there would be very little progress. Change is necessary in order for us to improve, refine, and further the assignment given to be accomplished in the earth. Change enables us to properly manage and be good stewards when adjustments are needed. For instance, when you develop to a certain financial level and a season of life arises where financial challenges occur, remember, royalty remains stable even during change. Royalty refuses to become an emotional wreck. People who learn to manage change well are peaceful, secure and optimistic where those who do not are stressed, fearful, and negative. I know

God said, "I am the Lord your God and I change not" (Malachi 3:6-8). However, I have a news flash- He never said that things wouldn't change for YOU. He's requiring you to become comfortable at being uncomfortable. He's constantly watching how you manage seasons of change.

 If you're concerned about things remaining the *same, you will be consistently disappointed.* Change will move us out of places we have been in longer than we should, to get us to the place and around the people He desires for us to be. So, remember the next time you're confronted with change, tell yourself,
"It's time for my next to make its arrival, I'm built for change and I was made to handle this!'"

7. ROYALTY REQUIRES RIGHT THINKING

You will keep him in perfect peace whose mind is stayed on you, because he trusts in you. (Isaiah 26:3)

It has been stated that the human brain can have anywhere between 12,000-60,000 thoughts a day and about 70% of them are believed to be negative. That's the reason why it is so vital that you take responsibility for **WHAT** you are thinking and **HOW** you are thinking.

Thoughts fuel your actions. They drive your passions and desires. Thoughts determine your outlook concerning yourself and others. That's why it is so important that you take personal inventory of what you set your thoughts upon. The mind is where you imagine, think, process and visualize your thoughts. It's where you develop your concepts and your beliefs. Scripture tell us in (Proverbs 23:7) "For as a man thinks in his heart (sub-conscious-mind) so is he".

Your mind is extremely powerful. It can actually present something that's not physically real, believe something that's not true and be fearful of something you should be in faith about. Having been born and raised in the world, your mind has become fashioned by this world's system. That's why it's important for you to take responsibility of your thoughts as well as what you allow through your "gates" (eyes and ears). Your mind was given to serve you, not you serving your mind. Without putting responsibility to work in this area, you will experience marginal success at best, when you were truly designed to win! Remember, when Satan tempted Jesus it was an attack not on his flesh but on His mind, which has the potential to control His flesh.

Thoughts are simply silent words and the word is exactly what Jesus used to defeat satan.

Luke 4:1-13 NIV
[1] Jesus, full of the Holy Spirit, left the Jordan and was led by the Spirit into the wilderness, [2] where for forty days he was tempted by the devil. He ate nothing during those days, and at the end of them he was hungry. [3] The devil said to him, "If you are the Son of God, tell this stone to become bread." [4] Jesus answered, "It is written: 'Man shall not live on bread alone.'" [5] The devil led him up to a high place and showed him in an instant all the kingdoms of the world. [6] And he said to him, "I will give you all their authority and splendor; it has been given to me, and I can

give it to anyone I want to. [7] If you worship me, it will all be yours." [8] Jesus answered, "It is written: 'Worship the Lord your God and serve him only." [9] the devil led him to Jerusalem and had him stand on the highest point of the temple. "If you are the Son of God," he said, "throw yourself down from here. [10] For it is written: "'He will command his angels concerning you to guard you carefully; [11] they will lift you up in their hands, so that you will not strike your foot against a stone." [12] Jesus answered, "It is said: 'Do not put the Lord your God to the test." [13] When the devil had finished all this tempting, he left him until an opportune time.

WOW!! Did you see that? The word is so powerful that when applied to our lives, it will cause thoughts which were overwhelming you, to flee when you speak and believe them by faith. Therefore, we must be transformed by the renewing of our minds.
(Romans 12:2). Many are trying to live the Kingdom life without transforming their minds. Somewhere they have taken on a false concept that God will just make everything new without any effort on their part. *They want*

*a new life, new family, new marriage, new career,
new results and new outcomes without any
requirements on their part.* **They're born again
but not transformed. They have a new spirit
but an old mind.** They operate from old
thinking and old believing. It's like having a
new car with an old GPS system. No matter
where you program it to go, it will keep taking
you to the previous destinations. You will only
go to what is familiar and never experience
what is destined ahead.

(Philippians 2:5) "Let this mind be in you that
was also in Christ Jesus.

When we allow the mind and words of Christ
to shape, instruct, train and transform our
thinking, we become unstoppable!

Here are a few points I would like to encourage
you with;

* Be responsible to give your mind a strategic
and purposeful focus.

*Feed your mind with healthy pictures of your coming future, not the outdated replays of your unhealthy past.

*Feed your mind with faith food consistently.

*Be intentional about bringing every thought captive to the obedience of Christ…
(2 Corinthians 10:5)

*Don't allow your thoughts to lead you, instead be led by your thoughts which should be inspired by your spirit man.

*Deal with negative, defeating, self-sabotaging thoughts, painful memories and distortions of truth. Remember that your mind is like a field ready for planting.

*Lastly, inspect all seeds prior to their entry into your mind because the quality of your harvest will depend on the quality of the seed.

8. ROYALTY REQUIRES STRENGTH IN THE POSITION

Use your power and position wisely
Dr DeNae LeMay

The culture of any nation will determine the direction of that nation.

Many believe that our nation is headed in a direction where many entitle minded individuals are positioning themselves more on the receiving end of benefits and less on the responsible end. When I accepted the assignment to assist my husband, Dr. Stacy LeMay, in establishing Champion Kingdom Center, over 13 years ago, little did I know of all the joys and challenges that were to come. Pastoring has been one of the greatest assignments (next to my husband and children) of my life. To see lives come from darkness into light, from being bound to being set free. Nothing brings me greater joy than to see individuals transition from being isolated, into being a part of a family and helping the voiceless become as bold as Lions. I think that is so awesome!

Over these many years we have observed many who have hungered for truth and have experienced great victory.
Yet, we have also witnessed those who want;

-Help without change
-Relationship without commitment
-Conversation without truth
-Their own desires without His will
-His intervention without their investment.

In other words, they want Benefits, Privilege and Position without Responsibility.

Today, we are seeing more who are eager for the star studded position, but retreat when it's time for responsibility.

Every meaningful Position has worth, value and responsibility attached to it. It's very much like water, as you don't get the water without getting wet. **Much like water and wet is a package deal, position and responsibility are a package deal and can't be separated.**

They are necessary, beneficial and require proper management. Whenever someone refuses to accept responsibility, a vacancy of leadership is created and could potentially cause deficits or delays in progress. As one who represents Royalty, always be cognitive of this fact, the position you hold in God's Kingdom is highly valuable and you are necessary to His ultimate plan.

You were created to be His representative in the earth and like yeast impacts the dough, you were designed to IMPACT the world. *You were commissioned to infiltrate the systems of the world, recreate the culture, legislate laws in alignment with Heaven so that His glory can cover the earth!* Always remember that all positions have power attached to them. Be sure that you use your power and position wisely! King Saul choose to use power and position unwisely and it not only cost him the Kingdom, but also his life! Don't abdicate your responsibility. Your position was entrusted to you by the King. What you do, what you say and how you behave affects everyone and everything around you. Remember, it's never about you only! It's about those whom you have been sent to impact and influence.

NEVER FORFEIT YOUR POSITION!

The price of regaining trust and position is always greater than it cost to lose it!

CHAPTER 8

IT'S YOURS FOR THE TAKING!

If you are going to be inclined to take something,
Let it be responsibility
- *Dr DeNae LeMay*

At the beginning of 2016, I heard the Spirit of the Lord say, "It's time for my women to ARISE, EMERGE and DO! Those who will hear and obey this word I will allow them to SEE what others cannot and HEAR what many will not! This word became my theme all year long. I shared this with any and everyone who would listen and today I am witnessing the fruit of this word in many women's lives. As I look around, I see women who are stepping out of the shadows and into the light. This is glorious to behold. I see courageous women who understand that the assignment is not limited within the four walls. They have become convinced that it's within the systems. I'm excited to see women ARISING all over the world, but there's room for so many more. There's actually a place with your name assigned to it. Yes, there is room for your gift, talent and ability within the system. There are women who are waiting for you to cancel fear, dismiss doubt, silence the negative chatter and soar. You're unique and one of a kind design is so needed, I can hear destiny calling out to you,

"Take your place Queen, Royalty is your inheritance. Due to delays, your throne has been vacant and awaiting your arrival!"

Like Queen Esther, *Esther 4:14, "you have been called into the Kingdom for such a time as this!"* Your gifts, talents, abilities, passions, height, eyes, voice are all for the purpose assigned to your life.

That is why we must be prepared and able to respond upon request. We must be prepared with wisdom, virtue, boldness, faith and revelation in order to give an answer to the issues our society is facing today. Families, marriages, men, women, businesses, schools and government are all experiencing problems with no sustainable solutions. This leads to frustration and despair. As Kingdom Carriers, we know that we have the answers within us. We carry solutions in which society is pressing to hear.

Luke 16:16 NIV
[16] "The Law and the Prophets were proclaimed until John. Since that time, the good news of the Kingdom of God is being preached, and everyone is forcing their way into it.

Therefore, we need women who;
- Value their Kingdom assignment greater than their own desires.
- Are willing to stand out and BE different in order to MAKE a difference.
- Are willing to use their influence in leading others by truth and integrity.
- Will demonstrate leadership by being a model and example others can follow.
- Are willing to be misunderstood in order to become His messenger.

Today, you have the opportunity unlike any other time in history to ARISE, EMERGE and

DO all that the King has placed within your heart to do! He has fashioned you and equipped you with unique gifts, talents and abilities in order to do your assignment. You are an intelligent, determined, caring, multi-tasking woman of God, who loves putting your hand and heart into something and watching it grow. The Father loves His daughters. Remember, you're the apple of His eye. He has a special purpose and plan for each of us. There's no need to be jealous, envious, angry, worried, fearful, anxious nor doubtful. He knows the plans He has for you. He's wanting you to trust Him, obey Him and allow Him to lead you into victory. When you address "the holes within your soul" you could look forward to the future through the eyes of victory. **The pursuit is always about your Father's business**. *It's about His Kingdom and His will being done on earth as it is in Heaven.*

In closing, I encourage you with this...

Royal daughter of the King.
I know it gets challenging at times, but you must continue pursuing the crown no matter what, being assured that you were born for

such a time and that you were built for this!
Lastly, *know that your Heavenly Father will never leave nor forsake you, and just as he chose Queen Esther, He believes that*
You are The "ONE."

Surely God has a plan for His people and for you. Therefore, remain in passionate pursuit and receive your crown! Never forgetting that **You are Royalty!**

Live Royally,

Dr. DeNae LeMay

_____

_____

_____

_____

_____

_____

_____

_____

_____

_____

_____

_____

_____

_____

_____

_____

_____

_____

_____

_____

_____

_____

_____

_____

_____

_____

_____

_____

_____

_____

_____

_____

_____

_____

_____

_____

_____

_____